CASTLES

CASTLES

DONALD SOMMERVILLE

Grange
BOOKS

Published by Grange Books
An Imprint of Grange Books PLC
The Grange
Grange Yard
London SE1 3AG

This edition published in 1995

ISBN 1-85627-629-5

Produced by Bison Books Ltd
Kimbolton House
117A Fulham Road
London SW3 6RL

Printed in China

Page 1: Qalat Ibn Maan, Palmyra

Pages 2-3: Chateau Gaillard towers above the Seine in Normandy near Les Andelys. It was begun in 1196 by Richard the Lionheart of England and may in part have been designed by him personally. It incorporated features similar to those in some of the Crusading castles in the Holy Land with which Richard would have been familiar. It stands on a cliff spur some 300 feet above the river. Unusually for such a major fortress of this period it was captured, after a particularly bitter siege, in 1203-4. Catapults, battering rams, siege towers and undermining by sappers were all employed. A luckless group of non-combatants sent out of the castle by the garrison spent a dreadful winter trapped outside the walls and were said to have been reduced to eating first their dogs and then their children.

Page 4: The castle at Corfe in Dorset was a royal stronghold built on the site of an ancient ring fort. The massive keep was probably begun in the early twelfth century by Henry I. It was King John's favorite castle and he built a very fine suite of apartments here. John found a variety of uses for Corfe, imprisoning his wife here in 1212, and later hiding his crown and other treasures within the walls. Henry III and Richard II are among the later monarchs who commissioned alterations.

Page 5: Conisbrough in South Yorkshire was probably first fortified in the years shortly after the Norman Conquest by William de Warenne, one of the principal lords of William the Conqueror. The structure was entirely rebuilt in the later part of the twelfth century by Hamelin Plantagenet, half-brother of Henry II, who married the de Warenne heiress in 1163. The photograph shows the ruins of the inner ward and the great buttressed keep.

CONTENTS

INTRODUCTION

"The house of every man is to him as his Castle and Fortresse, as well for his defence against injury and violence, as for his repose."

Castles are principally associated with the medieval and early modern period of European history, and it is generally and correctly understood that they were the strongholds and residences of the kings and their feudal vassals, the knights, who ruled the land, taxed and exploited the peasants, fought the wars and defended the realm. A well-known maxim of English Law says that "an Englishman's home is his castle," and the quotation above, one of the earliest-known statements of this principle, by one Sir Edward Coke, who was chief justice in the early seventeenth century, neatly sums up the combination of military and domestic functions that a castle was expected to fulfil.

Dictionary definitions of the word "castle," generally describe a fortified building or group of buildings, usually also a residence, and having such features as thick sheer walls, battlements, and perhaps a ditch or moat. In some languages also the analogous word (like the French *château*) has come to mean principally the later development of the castle to become the grand country mansion. It is interesting, too, that in English castle once also meant village, the home and refuge of a community, not merely the property of a single family.

Various types of fortification were known in different parts of the Ancient world, in the Assyrian empire more than 1000 years before Christ for example. In somewhat more recent times, Alexander the Great and Julius Caesar fought in a number of notable sieges among their many important battles. However, the real development of what we now understand as castles began in the medieval period. The earliest castles are often said to have appeared in France, perhaps in the tenth century at places like Blois or Saumur, and spread with the Normans to Britain in the eleventh century, by which time they had also become common elsewhere. This is a simplification, but a useful one, of what was in fact a complicated historical process in which similar social and military changes were taking place in many areas and at roughly at the same time.

The form which these early castles generally took was simple also. A mound of earth or *motte* would be excavated and topped with a wooden fort (which in time was enlarged and built of stone as a *keep*) which would be the stronghold and residence of the lord. Alongside this would be the *bailey*, a larger enclosure (again at first protected by a wooden palisade) with accommodation for tenants and underlings, and sufficient space to pen animals when attack was threatened.

The processes by which castles became ever larger, more elaborate and more

Previous page: Schloss Neuschwanstein in Bavaria, commissioned by Ludwig II, "Mad King Ludwig" of Bavaria, was begun in 1869 to a design partly by Eduard Riedel and partly by C. Jank who was more used to designing sets for Wagner's operas. King Ludwig built a series of castles based around various themes. Neuschwanstein was inspired by the operas of Wagner and the German folk tales which they embodied.

Above: The Château de Chenonçeau and the River Cher. The 200-foot long Galerie over the Cher was commissioned by Catherine de Medici in the mid-sixteenth

century. The history of Chenonçeau earlier in that century is as rich a tale of royal trickery as one could wish for. The estate was acquired by a leading royal tax collector, Thomas Bohier, in 1521 after the previous owners had been helped on the way to hard times. After Bohier and his wife died a few years later, King François I confiscated the castle from the family in settlement of a concocted tax bill. Not content with this, Henri II then invalidated the first transaction and confiscated the château again to 'sell' it (no money changed hands) to his mistress Diane de Poitiers. After Henri in turn died, his widow, Catherine de Medici, took her revenge by

having Diane evicted. In 1940-42, during World War II, the border between the part of France occupied by the Germans and the puppet Vichy Republic ran along the river with one end of the Galerie in each zone. The room is said to have served many escaping from the Germans as the crossing point between the zones.

Above right: The ruins of Corfe Castle. By the time of the Civil War Corfe had passed to a Royalist, Sir John Banks, whose wife briefly led its defense for the king before it was captured and demolished in 1646.

hugely expensive to meet changes in military technology were complex and will be detailed more fully in the captions of individual pictures in this book. Matters of structural engineering and the geometry of fields of fire could be calculated scientifically but there was also always an element of artistry in adapting these to take best account of the features of a particular site.

Gradually, as cannon and other gunpowder weapons developed and as societies across Europe became less subject to constant violence, the design of noble residences and the forms of military architecture began to diverge. The structure of castles began to lay greater emphasis on the comfort of the owners both in the internal arrangement and in such matters as the provision of external windows. Fortification took a new route too, with ditches and bastions and

emplaced artillery proliferating to keep an attacker at a distance; for by the sixteenth century even the thickest stone walls could rapidly be battered down by a well organized siege train. Many of medieval England's castles met just this fate in the Civil War of the 1640s.

The new type of castle, the noble residence, though built with fewer and fewer genuine defensive features, continued to flourish, and arguably reached a peak with costly renovations and new eccentric extravagances in the nineteenth century. There was "Mad King Ludwig" of Bavaria who emptied his treasury building fabulous edifices like Neuschwanstein. Or, if you prefer a homelier tale, turn to the English industrialist, Sir George Bullough, building a fantasy castle far from the public view on a remote island in Scotland, who thought appearances so important that he was pleased to pay his English workmen a bonus provided they wore kilts.

Castles by their nature were usually built on splendid sites and this, combined with their varying forms designed to meet changing military and social requirements, makes them a handsome subject for a pictorial study like this one. Their stories are no less dramatic and interesting – great sieges and dark deeds in the dungeons on the one hand, and the fascinating social history of their owners and their servants on the other. This book can be little more than an introduction to this rich and rewarding subject but I hope that it captures something of the grandeur and romance that make castles so intriguing.

RULING THE TOWNS

Castles were designed to dominate their surroundings and nowhere is this more evident to the onlooker than at the heart of those towns and cities whose central feature is an ancient castle. Many such cities were once capitals and may have owed their selection as such to the security derived from positioning the royal stronghold on an impregnable site. The Hohensalzburg in Vienna and the Hradcany in Prague are two of the most famous of Europe's capital city/castle pairings. Some, like Moscow's Kremlin or Delhi's Red Fort, are not even sited on particularly dominating ground, but their influence on the development of their respective cities and countries was nonetheless all too clear – especially to the unfortunate prisoners, traitors and victims of court intrigues who found their ends in their darkest dungeons or on the executioners' scaffolds.

Some castles at the heart of capital cities were built as the focus and center of alien rule – the Tower of London is perhaps the best example, established by William the Conqueror early in his successful attempts to consolidate his hold on his new English crown. Castles would certainly bring economic development to a town and its surroundings, but at the risk of being caught up in rebellion or royal displeasure. Sometimes the castle and town went their separate ways for a time – Edinburgh in Scotland was captured by Bonnie Prince Charlie's Jacobite rebels in 1745 and, while they danced and celebrated at the royal palace of Holyrood House at one end of the city, the castle resolutely held out for King George at the other.

At times it is difficult to tell what is a castle in its own right and what is merely a feature in the defenses of a city – the Castel Sant'Angelo in Rome is one illustration of this. In other cases it is hard to know when a group of fortified buildings becomes a castle, or at what point it becomes a defended town or village. The *bastides* (usually translated as fortified villages) of southwest France, fought over by England and France in the Hundred Years War, are well known in this category. This book does not attempt to achieve a precise definition of what is a castle – taking the view that castles are what people generally think they are – but concentrates instead on their exciting and romantic history. Not for nothing is the castle on the hill above the town such a regular feature in drama and fiction. The true stories are equally as absorbing.

Page 11: The Round Tower at Windsor Castle is based on a twelfth century shell keep on its motte, but was extensively restored and rebuilt in the nineteenth century, as was much of the remainder of what is now one of Britain's great royal palaces. There are numerous royal associations with the site. Henry II built extensively in what is now the upper ward and many of his walls still stand. Windsor stood a tough siege in 1216 during a French invasion when it was held for King John by his mercenary captain Engelard de Cigogné. Edward III spent the truly massive sum of £50,000 in the mid-fourteenth century transforming Windsor into one of the greatest royal palaces of Europe and attempting to make it a fitting home for his newly-created Order of the Garter, and George IV spent over £1 million on the work he commissioned from Sir Jeffrey Wyatville in the early nineteenth century.

Pages 12-13: The Tower of London seen from Tower Bridge. The central keep of the Tower, known as the White Tower, was constructed by William the Conqueror to protect and control the city. Down the years the Tower has served many functions, notably as the most famous prison in England, and has often been the execution ground for those suspected or convicted of treason. It is the home, even now, of a flock of ravens and tradition has it that when the ravens leave the Tower will fall. The Crown Jewels are displayed here along with part of the magnificent collection of the Royal Armouries.

Above: Norwich Castle viewed from the south. In 1067 William the Conqueror ordered William fitz Osbern (see also Chepstow, page 86) to build a fortification at Norwich which was then one of the principal towns of England. Over 100 houses were demolished to make room to build this first Norwich castle, which had a particularly large motte. The present structure is based around a keep constructed by Henry I. This was extended and altered over the years, but was completely reconstructed in the 1830s when the exterior was refaced and the interior gutted. The exterior reconstruction is believed to have been a reasonably accurate restoration of many early features.

Above: The castle at Caernarvon was begun under the orders of Edward I of England in 1283 to protect the English borough he wanted to establish as part of his plan for controlling north Wales. Caernarvon was intended to be the seat of royal government and to be the palace of the Prince of Wales. The castle's long curtain wall is strengthened by a series of towers with a rather unusual additional feature of further small towers set on top of these. Inside, the arrangement is divided by a crosswall, making an inner and outer ward. Like most of Edward's castles in Wales, Caernarvon is believed to have been designed by James of St George, a noted military engineer from Savoy.

Overleaf, left: An aerial view of Beaumaris Castle, Anglesey. Beaumaris was also started under Edward I to further his control of his Welsh conquests. The inner walls were begun in 1295 to a design by James of St George and the outer curtain was added from 1316 by Nicholas de

Derneford, probably following St George's original scheme. The moat (appearing as a brown colour in this view, around the top and right of the castle) originally extended all round the defenses. The strongest parts of the fortifications were the keep-gatehouses of the inner ward. This combined structure, rather than a separate central keep, is a characteristic of the design of many English castles.

Overleaf right: Lincoln was one of the earliest castles built in England by William the Conqueror from 1068. The oldest structure was placed in the same position as part of the city's ancient Roman walls but these were buried under the spoil from the new ditches which were dug. The original wooden motte had been replaced in stone by the second decade of the twelfth century. In the civil war of the 1140s Lincoln was an important focus. It was first seized by Rannulf, Earl of Chester. who then successfully negotiated joint rights of ownership with King Stephen. This seems

to be the explanation for the fact that there are two mottes inside Lincoln Castle, where the present Observatory Tower and the Lucy Tower now stand. Lucy was Rannulf's mother. The king and Rannulf then quarrelled again, Stephen being wounded and held prisoner for a time when his attack on Lincoln failed. Stephen finally regained the castle two years later when he managed to imprison Rannulf in turn. Lincoln was one of the few castles which was successfully held, by Sir Nicholas de la Haye, for King John and then his young son Henry III in 1216-17. Within a hundred years of this Lincoln's defenses were beginning to be neglected. By the time of the Civil War in 1644 it was taken in less than a day by Parliamentary attackers. That the castle was kept even in basic repair was because of its continuing role as a court house (which it still is). The association with law and order was still greater in Victorian times when part of the premises was also a prison.

Above: Colchester in Essex, seen from the northeast. Colchester was one of the most massive stone keeps built by William the Conqueror. It is in fact sited on the remains of a temple dedicated to another conqueror of England, the Roman Emperor Claudius. Some of the Roman bricks were re-used in the Norman building. Like many of the other castles featured in this book, it changed hands (in fact more than once) during the rebellion against King John in 1216-17. After falling into disrepair the castle was sold for demolition in 1683, but the new owner gave up this project after removing the top two of the original four stories.

Above: A view of the south interior of
Warwick Castle. These buildings,
overlooking the River Avon on their other
side, were the principal domestic
accommodation of the castle and have
been much rebuilt over the centuries.
Warwick was originally built in 1068 by
William I. The original motte and shell keep
were behind the position from which this
picture was taken.

Overleaf: The river and east frontage of
Warwick Castle. The towers and gate-
house of the east side are the most
impressive sections of the building.
Nearest the camera is Caesar's Tower then
to the right the gate-house and right of that
Guy's Tower. The castle was owned by the
Beauchamp family, the Earls of Warwick,
whose fortunes prospered under Edward
III. The third earl, Thomas, was a founding
member of the Order of the Garter and his
son was responsible for much of the
building on the east front during the last
quarter of the fourteenth century. The
towers were built principally to provide
suitable lodging for the important retainers
whom lords were maintaining in increasing
numbers at their residences by this time.
Both towers have machicolations and a
guard room on their top floors, but their
aggressive appearance is belied by the
absence of arrow slits lower down. The
gate-house is perhaps more formidable. It
has an outer barbican which can be seen
through the trees in this photograph. This
encloses an open space which could be
fired upon from all sides. There were two
portcullises, further covered by murder
holes, and beyond the barbican was a
drawbridge over the ditch.

Left: Scarborough was begun around 1140 by William of Aumale during the anarchy of Stephen's reign, but in 1155 it was passed over to Henry II as part of his policy of acquiring private castles to check the power of his many over-mighty subjects. Scarborough Castle overlooks the sea, with cliffs on all sides, apart from one narrow approach. A wall and ditch further protect the landward side and Henry ordered the construction of a stone keep to overlook the entrance. This cost £650 and was built between 1157-69 under a mason called David Lardener. The keep and part of the wall of the inner bailey are shown in the photograph. The keep originally was some 30 metres (100 feet) tall. The site was strengthened further by the construction of a barbican during the reign of Henry III. Much of Scarborough's present ruined condition is owed to the damage inflicted during the Civil War when Parliamentary cannon battered the defenses.

Above: The ditch and gate of Edinburgh Castle is dominated by the Half Moon Battery above, which, as can clearly be seen from its gun ports, belongs to the age of cannon. Edinburgh Castle is set on a rocky crag in the middle of the city with only a single relatively level approach, to this gate. The present gate-house itself is ninteenth century. The open space of the esplanade, now best known as the theater for the annual military tattoos, would be dominated by fire from the battery. The oldest building that now exists within the extensive precincts of the castle is the twelfth century St Margaret's Chapel. Margaret was the queen of Malcolm Canmore in the eleventh century and it was her son, David I, who made Edinburgh Scotland's capital.

Overleaf: Stirling Castle was the focus of the struggles for Scotland's independence in the late thirteenth and early fourteenth centuries. It was surrendered to Edward I of England after a notable siege in 1304. The Battle of Bannockburn in 1314 was fought within sight of its walls when Edward II's invading army was soundly defeated in an attempt to relieve Stirling before a date by which its garrison had promised to surrender. In accordance with his policy, Robert the Bruce dismantled the castle after its surrender after Bannockburn. The existing buildings are now mostly fifthteenth and sixteenth century, including the fine Renaissance palace built for James V in the 1540s. In more recent times the castle has been used as a barracks and museum.

Left: The Neckar River and Heidelberg Castle. Heidelberg was the capital of the Rhineland state of the Palatinate whose rulers were Prince Electors of the Holy Roman Empire. Their medieval fortress was converted into a Renaissance palace in the later sixteenth and early seventeenth centuries. It was badly damaged in wars with France at the end of the seventeenth century and has never been substantially repaired.

Above: The walls of the fortified city of Carcassonne are believed to date back originally as far as the fifth century and to have been built by the Visigoths. The town was an important stronghold of the Cathar heretics in the 13th century and was captured by Simon de Montfort during the Albigensian Crusade. There are two concentric ramparts with an open walkway between them. There are 52 towers reinforcing the walls and the two gates are more heavily fortified still, each with a portcullis and drawbridge. The walls and battlements were extensively restored, not always with exact attention to historical accuracy, in the second half of the nineteenth century under the guidance of Viollet-le-Duc.

Left: A section of the defenses of Castel Sant'Angelo in Rome. The original major building on this site was the mausoleum of the Roman Emperor Hadrian. This was converted into a fortress by Pope Leo IV to defend against Saracen attacks in the ninth century. Further extension and development followed over many years. The most important changes were commissioned by Pope Alexander VI (the Borgia pope) at the end of the fifthteenth century, when he had the architect Antonio da Sangallo add bastions to the round corner towers to make them more defensible in the age of gunpowder. Pope Clement VII endured a long siege by the forces of the Emperor Charles V in Sant'Angelo in 1527. The photograph gives a good besiegers' eye view of the machicolations on the round towers. These overhanging sections of the battlements with holes below them, allowed weapons to be fired down or boiling liquids or other items to be dropped on attackers at the base of the walls. These features would become less important to defenses as the use of gunpowder became more widespread.

Right: Castilo de la Mota was built to protect the important trading center of Medina del Campo in the Asturias, Spain. Like many Spanish castles its most obvious feature is a dominating keep, crowned as the photograph shows with machicolations and bartizans (the small battlemented turrets). There was probably a castle on this site from at least the twelfth century, but the present structure was built in 1440-80, initially to a design by Fernando de Carreño and commissioned by John II. The castle became notorious over the years as a prison. Among those held here was Cesare Borgia (son of Pope Alexander VI) but he escaped with the aid of a smuggled file and rope, cutting his cell bars and climbing down into the dry moat.

Sunset over the Hradcany Palace in Prague. There has been a fortification on this site since at least around 870 in the early days of the Premyslid dynasty. Later, this also became the seat of the Bishops of Prague and their St Vitus Cathedral is at the heart of the Hradcany today. The citadel today follows the lines established by fortifications built around 1140.

The Hradcany viewed from across the
Charles Bridge. In its later history the
Hradcany was an important Hapsburg
imperial palace. The famous
"defenestration of Prague," one of the
incidents causing the Thirty Years War of
1618-48, took place here. The present
buildings owe most to the rebuilding
commissioned in the baroque style from
the architect Nicolo Pacassi by the
Empress Maria Theresa in the eighteenth
century. From 1918, and again after 1945,
the Hradcany became the seat of the
government of Czechoslovakia.

Above: Fort St Elmo, Valletta. Malta. When the Knights of St John were expelled from the Holy Land they went to Rhodes, but were conquered there in turn by the Turks in 1522. In 1530 the Holy Roman Emperor granted the island of Malta to the Knights. St Elmo stands on a promontory between the island's two principal harbors, Grand Harbor and Marsam, and as soon as the Knights arrived they built a battery here, designed by Pedro Prado. In the Great Siege of 1565 it was the first target of the forces of Suleiman the Magnificent and held out in an epic struggle for five weeks, being finally captured in ruins when virtually the whole garrison was dead. The present fort is based around the replacement built by Laperelli in 1567, like its predecessor a five-pointed star fort.

Right: Fort St Angelo seen from Valletta. St Angelo stands in what is now Vittoriosa, one of the Three Cities, but was known as Birgu when the Knights first arrived. An Arab fort existed here as early as 828, and later a small palace which was used by the Grand Masters of the Knights. The present fort is seventeenth century and designed by Carlos de Grunenberg. For a time before and during World War II, the Royal Navy's Mediterranean HQ was here. The fort was one of the navy's 'stone frigates' (shore establishments officially listed as ships) and as HMS St Angelo it was hit by at least 70 German bombs.

Previous pages: Markab, now in Syria, was one of the great Crusader castles defending the northern frontier of the Kingdom of Jerusalem. The original massive stonework and range of towers protecting an already strong site are apparent even in its present ruined state. Richard the Lionheart visited Markab during the Third Crusade.

Above & Right: St Simeon's Basilica and the citadel at Aleppo, the seat of various successive local rulers in northern Syria. There was much building here commissioned by Nûr ad-dîn following an earthquake in 1157, and considerable changes thereafter at various times until the early 1500s. Aleppo was attacked by the Mongols in both 1260 and 1400.

Above: The Red Fort or Lal Qila in Delhi. This fabulous enclosure of palaces and gardens is surrounded by some 2¹/₂ km (1¹/₂ miles) of battlements and was the fortress and palace of the Mughal emperors. Shah Jehan, the builder of the Taj Mahal, moved his capital here in the seventeenth century but he was later deposed by his son Aurangzeb, who was the last Mughal truly to rule from Delhi. The Red Fort was once richly furnished and decorated but was stripped in the aftermath of the Indian Mutiny of 1857.

Right: Machu Picchu, the lost city of the Incas of Peru. The city is an elaborate and remarkable combination of fortresses and temples whose stonework is a marvel of craftsmanship. It was abandoned by the Incas before the Spanish arrived and so escaped the destruction visited on much of the rest of their culture. It was only found, or rather re-discovered, in 1911.

LORDS OF THE LAND

Castles were expressions of rule and naked military force, the harsh and unforgiving products of times, despite all our modern ills, far more violent and lawless, and generally uncomfortable than the present day. This can be hard to remember for the modern visitor to a pleasant rural castle on a bright summer day. Fine old stonework reflects on the still waters of the moat where ducks and ornamental carp swim languidly, and the invaders quietly crossing the drawbridge are strolling tourists armed only with their cameras.

Despite this appearance of calm these were the military barracks and arsenals, tax offices and court houses, food stores and cultural centers of those former times, built and maintained to govern and subdue and at times to protect. Their lords had rights over every aspect of the life of their vassals – in Scotland the traditional chilling description of this ultimate authority was of "pit and gallows" – and many used this power to the full.

In time this behavior became softened by processes of law, and the development of ideas of chivalry and courtly love. Certainly stories of castles are tinged with romance as well as brutality – Richard the Lionheart making a dramatic escape from imprisonment during his return from great exploits on crusade, for example. Richard was also one of the great castle builders – Château Gaillard towering above the Seine in Normandy was his finest – but the harsh reality is that his life was ended with a painful poisoned wound in a squalid and unimportant siege.

Such unpleasant facts should not deter the modern visitor from trying to imagine what life was like in castles in their heyday. They would certainly have been cold and draughty in winter, dark and damp all year round, but one cannot help feeling that in the good times their great halls would fill with noise and warmth, the rich smells of cooking would mask other odors, and fun and coarse good fellowship prevailed.

Above all, for the same modern visitor, there remains the austere beauty of their architecture, and the unquestionable attraction of their varied and handsome settings.

Previous page: Berkeley Castle was originally a motte and bailey construction which subsequently had a shell keep added enclosing the whole motte. It was much modified down the years with new ranges of domestic buildings being added over the area of the bailey. Berkeley is most famous for the gruesome murder of King Edward II, which took place in the dungeon in 1327. An additional horror related to this hideous event was that the castle's sewer ran through the dungeon.

Above: Maiden Castle is an Iron Age hill fort with an elaborate pattern of three successive rings of banks and ditches. Many of the sites later used for Norman and other castles took advantage of far older defensive structures like this. Maiden Castle is believed to have been fortified or at least inhabited in one way or another for perhaps 5000 years. It was stormed by a Roman legion commanded by the future Emperor Vespasian in AD 43.

Above: Although the local tourist authorities make much of the story, Tintagel Castle has no definite connection with the real personality who is now celebrated in the various legends of King Arthur. The first castle in the true sense was built on this rocky promontory by Reginald, Earl of Cornwall, in the twelfth century, but very little of this now remains. The current ruins owe most to a younger son of Henry III, Richard, Earl of Cornwall in the mid-thirteenth century and to the fourteenth century Black Prince who rebuilt part in his capacity as Duke of Cornwall.

Overleaf: Old Wardour Castle in Wiltshire is carefully arranged in a hexagonal plan around a central courtyard with the great hall positioned above the main entrance and would also originally have been surrounded by a similarly shaped bailey. It was built from 1393 by Lord Lovel. The stonework is finely detailed and finished, and various minor features reflect a fashionable French style of the time. Although it would have been garrisoned with the lord's retainers the castle says more about image and style than military strength.

Above: A royal license to build and fortify Herstmonceux Castle was granted in 1441 to a veteran of England's wars in France, Sir Roger Fiennes. Brick-built on a quadrilateral plan, it is of little military strength. Instead, many of its features clearly point toward the development of the Tudor style of country house in England. Herstmonceux is now the official residence of Britain's Astronomer Royal.

Right: The great tower at Orford in Suffolk was built by Henry II in 1165-73 at a cost of about £1400 (the king's annual income from his English possessions at this time was about £10,000). Originally the tower was set within a walled enclosure but only earthworks remain to mark this feature. Orford was built partly as a check on the power of the Earls of Norfolk, whose castle at Framlingham (featured in its slightly later guise overleaf) was nearby. Its polygonal form was a development from the original square style of keep, which had been found to be less effective in resisting battering from siege engines, and to provide less opportunity for flanking fire to be directed down at attackers.

Previous pages: The present Framlingham Castle was built around 1200 by the Bigod family who were Earls of Norfolk. It was one of the first to be built without a massive central keep, trusting instead to the strength of the enclosing wall. It was an important center for the rebellion against King John in 1216. In the sixteenth century Queen Mary began her campaign to reclaim the throne from Lady Jane Grey from here. An important feature of the defenses, which can still be seen, was a carefully calculated series of archery loops for both longbow and crossbow men, designed to provide overlapping layers of fire along any approach to the walls.

Above: Kenilworth is a good example of an eleventh century Norman castle greatly modified and extended in succeeding centuries. It was also extensively protected by water defenses added in the thirteenth century when it was one of Simon de Montfort's principal power bases in his struggle with Henry III. The greatest reconstruction was in the later fourteenth century when John of Gaunt built a great hall, said to be the finest in the land apart from Westminster, and other facilities in the ward inside the original curtain wall. The curtain wall appears in the photograph and light can be seen through the ornate windows of the now roofless hall. The tower to the right of the hall contained John of Gaunt's personal apartments. A later owner, who carried out further rebuilding, was the Earl of Leicester, favorite for a time of Elizabeth I. Kenilworth was bombarded and captured by Parliamentary forces during the Civil War.

Right: The late fourteenth century gatehouse at Donnington is the only part of the castle which still stands. This view is from what would have been the inside of the castle. Donnington was licensed in 1386 to Richard de Adderbury, a royal chamberlain. Its greatest fame came in the Civil War 260 years later when it held out against a siege for almost two years. The fourteenth century stonework was battered by the Parliamentary cannon but the real strength of the defense by then was a much more modern star-shaped earthwork incorporating bastions and batteries.

Above: Carisbrooke is built on what was
once the site of a Roman fort of around
AD300. Like many of the English castles in
this book it began its medieval life as a
motte of around 1070 and this had been
replaced by a stone keep and curtain wall
by the 1130s. The gate-house shown in the
photograph was built partly around 1335
and partly in the 1470s. In 1587-1600 the
outer defenses were substantially
modernized by Federico Giannibelli who
built angled bastions in the Italian style and
converted some existing sections to this
more modern shape. Charles I was
imprisoned in Carisbrooke during the Civil
War.

Above: The main entrance to Goodrich Castle. Goodrich has a commanding position above the Wye valley on the English-Welsh border and was one of the most important marcher castles, owned for a considerable time by the de Valence Earls of Pembroke. It has a twelfth century keep, but was extensively rebuilt around the start of the fourteenth century. The curved projection in the wall of the gate-house marks the apse of the castle chapel and above this would have been the constable's rooms. To the left of the gate-house is a lesser hall (the Great Hall is on the opposite side of the castle). The gate-house and bridge over the ditch was protected in turn by an outer barbican, out of picture to the right.

53

Left: Harlech Castle in Gwynedd was built in 1283-9 at a cost of £8000. Its design, by James of St George, is probably the most impressive of any of Edward I's great castles in Wales. Its defenses depend on a system of concentric curtain walls and a massive keep-gatehouse. The photograph shows the interior walls and turrets of the gate-house. A good demonstration of the power of resistance of castles was given by Harlech during the rebellion of Owain Glyndwr at the start of the fifteenth century. Harlech was cut off in 1400 and held out (admittedly against a moderate level of attack) until 1404 when some of the garrison deserted and by which time others had starved. When the surrender came only 20 defenders were left. Glyndwr's family was forced to surrender in turn to Henry IV after a siege in 1408-9 A further notable siege was during the Wars of the Roses when the castle was held for the Lancastrians from 1466-68. Even before all these great events the site of Harlech was famed in the folk-tale of the Mabinogion.

Above: The great tower and lord's chamber at Warkworth was built around 1380 in the unusual ground plan of a Maltese cross. It was a stronghold of the Percy family and was besieged and taken by Henry IV during their rebellion in 1405. The site at Warkworth is older than the tower which was built on top of an earlier motte. The curtain walls date from the thirteenth century.

Above: Raglan Castle, Gwent, was built by Sir William ap Thomas (who later took the name Herbert) in the 1430s. The photograph is taken from the lord's tower, known as the Yellow Tower of Gwent, and shows the massive keep-gatehouse, with its machicolations, on the right, and the decorated stonework around the large windows of the principal public rooms on the left. Raglan Castle underwent one of the most notable sieges of the Civil War, when it was held for the Royalists by the Earl of Worcester before being forced to surrender after an epic defense in 1646. Like many other castles captured in this war it was 'slighted' after its capture. That is to say, sufficient of its defenses were demolished as to make it indefensible on a later occasion.

Left: Detail of the wall defenses at Raglan Castle. By the time Raglan was built there was comparatively little likelihood of the castle coming under a full-scale siege or successfully resisting such an attack. Defense against sudden raids was still an issue, however, and gun-loops and the machicolations noted in the picture above were among the features employed to this end. The Yellow Tower also sits in a moat separated from the main sections of the castle.

Right: Braemar Castle is an L-plan tower house built on an old site by the Earl of Mar in 1628. It was badly damaged after being held for the Jacobites during the Glorious Revolution of 1689 and was left in poor repair. It was garrisoned by Hanoverian troops during and after the 1715 and 1745 Jacobite rebellions and remained an army post until 1797.

Above: The fifteenth century Castle
Campbell in Dollar Glen was once the
principal seat of the Campbell clan. It was
badly damaged during the Civil War, first
by Royalist attack and later by Cromwellian
forces. Castle Campbell was originally
known as Castle Gloom but had its name
changed by an act of the Scottish
parliament in 1490.

Right: Bothwell Castle from the southeast.
The thirteenth century donjon tower is the
most prominent feature of this construction.
Other buildings on the site are mainly from
the fourteenth and fifthteenth centuries. The
castle belonged to the Douglas family,
probably the most turbulent of the many
over-mighty subjects of the Scottish crown.

Above: Doune Castle, Perthshire, Scotland.
Castles remained in use as such for longer
in Scotland than in England. One form
which their design took was for a
residential tower for the lord to be built
alongside his great hall. Doune was
constructed in this way for the fourteenth
century 1st Duke of Albany, the ambitious
brother of King Robert III.

Above: Blarney Castle, County Cork, was built from 1446 by Cormac MacCarthy. Visitors come here to "kiss the Blarney stone" and acquire the voluble and persuasive speech said to be an Irish quality. The usage is said to have been coined by Elizabeth I in reference to evasive replies she kept receiving from the MacCarthy who owned the castle in her day. The stone itself is set in the battlements and the process of kissing it involves lying on one's back and leaning further back above the machicolations (which from a military-architectural point of view are particularly fine and well preserved).

Above: Trim in County Meath is the most
substantial of the Anglo-Norman castles in
Ireland. The keep was built in the 1190s
and the curtain walls some 30 years later.
Some of the Anglo-Norman castles in
Ireland were built on the same locations as
old forts or raths, but Trim instead is
situated close to an old monastic site. The
layout of the tower is interesting in that it
shows the developing separation between
the lord's private accommodation and the
more public Great Chamber. These are on
separate floors and are reached by
different staircases. For all its imposing
bulk Trim was not especially formidable
militarily. The towers make little provision
for providing flanking missile fire against
attackers on the walls and the walls
themselves are comparatively thin.

Above: The most notable feature of the castle of Falaise in Normandy is the round Talbot tower built by King Philip Augustus of France after he conquered the duchy in 1204. It stands beside the older square Anglo-Norman keep built by Henry I of England from 1123. This in turn was a replacement for a still older keep erected by William the Conqueror to guard the town of his birth. Henry I built between 20 and 30 major stone castles in Normandy alone, which were to perform an important strategic role in the Anglo-French conflicts up to the time of Philip Augustus and beyond.

Left: Saumur has a truly extensive history going back to Fulk Nerra, Count of Anjou in the tenth century. Saumur also features in a famous manuscript illustration in the Très Riches Heures of the Duc de Berri, where it is shown with an even greater proliferation of turrets chimneys, spires and other rooftop decorations than in this photo. Saumur came to Henry II of England as part of the dowry of Eleanor of Aquitaine, but was regained for France by Philip Augustus.

Above: The Château de Chaumont still has heavy circular corner towers, suggesting a powerful defensive system, but the many large windows tell a different story despite its imposing site on bluffs overlooking the Loire river. One famous change in the château's ownership took place in 1560 when Catherine de Medici, widow of the late King Henri II, forced the king's former mistress out of her favorite residence at Chenonçeau and into the supposedly less-attractive Chaumont. While she still owned the château, Catherine is said to have dabbled in sorcery and to have consulted a magic mirror for predictions of the future. From this she learned that her sons would all die before her and that her family, the Valois, would be supplanted by the descendants of Henry of Navarre. Other notable figures in the castle's history include Madame de Staël who was exiled here by Napoleon and found the summer heat oppressive.

Left: A typical small country château near La Roque Gageac in Périgord. This south-western part of France was the scene of much fighting between the English and French in the later stages of the Hundred Years War, and as well as the remains of castles and fortified manor houses, is known for the formidable hilltop bastides or fortified villages, one of the best known of which is Domme, which is within sight of where this photograph was taken across the Dordogne River.

Right: Haut Koenigsbourg has one of the most dramatic castles of Alsace, standing proudly amid the trees on a 2000-foot high hill. Although it is now in France its present structure is entirely German in style because it was restored in every detail as a fifteenth century fortress by Kaiser Wilhelm II of Germany in the years before World War I when Alsace was a German possession.

Left: The castle at Sirmione on the shores of Lake Garda was built by the Scaligeri family of Verona between 1290 and 1310. One of the main purposes of the castle was to control shipping on the lake and exact tolls. One section of the castle is a fortified dock providing a refuge for friendly vessels. The castle is arranged around the machicolated central tower seen in the photograph. The notched merlons on the battlements indicate the Scaligeri family's support for the Ghibelline party in Italy's troubles of the time. (Merlons are the upright parts of a parapet – the teeth – while the embrasures or spaces are more correctly called crenelles).

Above: Castel del Monte in Apulia was built from about 1240 by Frederick II, Hohenstaufen Holy Roman Emperor and King of Sicily. Some years before he had begun a policy of demolishing all private castles in his Italian possessions and replacing them with royal fortresses. Castel del Monte has been described as "one of the supreme achievements of medieval secular building." The overall scheme is octagonal and at each of the eight corners is an octagonal tower. The rooms in the towers are octagonal and the rooms between the towers are trapezoidal in shape, together making a most complicated and elaborate design. Architectural historians have compared elements of the design with other notable buildings, including the chapel of Charlemagne at Aachen and the Dome of the Rock in Jerusalem, both of which Frederick knew. The details of the building combine aspects of the classical and gothic styles. It is, however, rather small for a major royal fortress. It may have been designed as the central keep for a larger fortification which was never built or it may have been some sort of palace-cum-hunting lodge.

DEFENDING THE REALM

If some castles were built at the heart of an established lordship, many others were built on frontiers or in debatable land to protect against foreign incursions, or as expressions of alien rule.

The expansion of western Christendom of the eleventh through the fifteenth centuries by Crusades in the Orient and eastern Europe, and the *reconquista* in Spain was predictably accompanied by much castle building. Probably the most elaborate and militarily impressive castles ever built were the great fortresses of the Knights Templar and Knights Hospitaller protecting the borders of the crusading Kingdom of Jerusalem. The castles of the military-religious orders of Teutonic Knights in central and eastern Europe were scarcely less impressive.

The most notable castle builder of Britain's kings was Edward I of England who campaigned and built furiously in Wales and, with less lasting effect, in Scotland. Many of the ports of southern England also have notable castles, this time to defend against the threat of foreign invasion from France. Every land and sea frontier of those times is studded with such strongholds.

There is little gentleness in the design of the crusading castles. They are as brutal and militaristic as their builders, and the castles of ports and borders elsewhere are scarcely less powerful. When they were built they could indeed laugh a siege to scorn, unless their garrisons were weakened from within by treachery or some other cause. Soon they would be overtaken by the development of a gentler type of society and the new military technology of gunpowder, but in their time they reigned supreme.

Right: The massive stonework of the chapel at Krak des Chevaliers gives a clue to the great strength of the building. Krak was the greatest of the Crusader fortresses and the stronghold of the Knights of the Hospital of St John.

Overleaf: Krak des Chevaliers seen from the west. The site was first occupied by Crusaders under Tancred of Antioch in 1109. The knights took over an older fortification on the site and modified it in the 1140s, but the main parts of the structure surviving into modern times date from the early thirteenth century following works carried out after an earthquake in 1202. Krak was attacked on at least 12 occasions and never fell to assault. The remaining tiny garrison of Hospitaller knights surrendered it to Sultan Baibars in 1271 only when they received a forged letter purporting to come from their superiors. The defenses of Krak are based around a series of concentric curtain walls, strengthened against assault by provision for flanking fire from a series of great towers, and overlooked and covered by fire from the inner rings. Note, too, how the walls of the inner curtain slope outwards substantially at the base. This was a precaution to make undermining more difficult.

Page 74: One of the most famous defensive features of any castle is the gorge at the Crusading castle of Sahyun (also known as Saône) in Syria. This is man-made, cut from the rock to defend the eastern flank of the castle, leaving only the central pinnacle to carry a narrow bridge to a gate. The cutting is some 90 feet (27 metres) deep and 60 feet (18 metres) wide.

Page 75: The south wall at Sahyun, showing how much of the rest of the site has great natural strength without additional excavations. Before the Crusaders came to Sahyun it had already been fortified by the Byzantines. The keep was built from the old Byzantine castle. Sahyun was captured by Saladin in 1188 after a fierce bombardment by siege engines when the garrison had already been depleted by battlefield losses.

Left: Safita in southern Syria, seen from the west. Safita sits like many another castle on a rocky mountain spur. Its outer defenses have largely been covered by more modern building, but the massive keep remains. Its early history is a little obscure but it had become a Templar fortress by the last quarter of the twelfth century. An attack by the otherwise virtually all-conquering Saladin was fought off in 1188, but it finally fell to the Moslems in 1271, shortly before Krak des Chevaliers.

Above: The great castle at Marienburg (now Malbork) was the headquarters of the Teutonic Knights in their days of power in the fourteenth century when they ruled much of what is now Poland. The Teutonic Knights had begun their activities in the Holy Land like the other orders of the Hospital and the Temple, but they had soon begun to concentrate their activities in eastern Europe where the heathen were more accessible and less formidable. Various of the Grand Masters of the Order added new buildings at Marienburg during the fourteenth century until the river frontage of the castle exceeded 500 metres (550 yards). Like many of the Order's other castles, it combines many of the religious features of a monastery with the military requirements of a fortress. In 1410 the then Grand Master took the castle's cannon off to battle and a resounding defeat by the Poles at Tannenberg. King Vladislas then used the castle's cannon against it in an unsuccessful two-month siege. Later in the century the Order had to pledge the castle (and others) to their own mercenaries in lieu of unpaid wages. The mercenaries then revolted and sold the castle to the Poles. The Order, in decline since Tannenberg, never recaptured it. The castle was much restored during the nineteenth century but was badly damaged by shelling during World War II and again subsequently repaired.

Above: Dover Castle stands on a site that has been fortified for over 2000 years. A hill fort stood here in Iron Age times, the Romans had a signal station here and the Anglo-Saxons a fortified burh. William the Conqueror came here immediately after his victory at Hastings in 1066 and had work on a castle begun even before he moved on to capture London. The inner ward and keep shown in the photograph are largely the product of the 1180s, protecting the port that was an important link between the French and English territories of Henry II. This work cost around £7000 and was undertaken to the design of one Maurice the Engineer. The gate on the left is closely guarded by twin towers and there are a further 12 towers strengthening the perimeter of the curtain wall. The keep has walls of 5-6 metres thick (17-21 feet), but was also built with such attention to comfort as a piped water system! The castle has been much altered over the years with adaptations to permit the mounting of modern artillery taking place even as late as the Victorian era. It was a military headquarters again in World War II. The most famous attack on the castle was in 1215-16 when Hubert de Burgh and a garrison of 140 knights and a larger force of men-at-arms successfully held out against a French invasion.

Right: Bodiam Castle in East Sussex has a handsome setting in its moat. Bodiam's builder was Sir Edward Dalyngrigge, a veteran of England's wars in France, where he had made his fortune. He was given his license to crenellate Bodiam on 21 October 1385, supposedly to protect the locality against French raids up the navigable River Rother close by. Bodiam is one of the earliest castles in Europe to be fitted with gun loops as part of the defenses, but despite this, it is not particularly formidable. The interior is carefully subdivided into various suites of public and private rooms. The tower nearest the camera in the photograph contains what would have been Sir Edward's private apartments. The main entrance to the castle was originally across a bridge with a right angled turn through outer defenses (on the opposite side, not shown here) which compelled any attacker to expose his right, unshielded side to the defenders. A more recent owner of the castle was Lord Curzon, the noted early twentieth century politician, who had considerable restoration work carried out.

Left: Alnwick was originally built as a motte with two baileys in the eleventh century, possibly by Gilbert de Tesson who was standard bearer to William the Conqueror at the Battle of Hastings. It became the seat of the Percy family in 1309. The photograph shows the Hotspur gate, named after perhaps the most famous of the family, who was a noted fighter in the turbulent history of the English and Scots border and appears also in Shakespeare's Henry IV. The Scottish King William the Lion besieged Alnwick twice, being captured on the second occasion in 1174 by a relieving force.

Above: Ludlow Castle in Shropshire on England's Welsh border, built on a cliff above a river. The single gate tower dates from about 1100 and the Great Hall and other parts of the structure from the late thirteenth century. Although there are various towers in the design they seem not to be sited to assist the defense of the castle but to have been built principally to provide accommodation. Ludlow is the focus of much of the action in a famous story, The Romance of Fulk Fitzwarine, a twelfth century tale of sieges and combats before the castle walls between the castle's owners and their local enemies. In the best tradition of such stories it includes a lady helping her lover escape from the dungeons, his secret return to capture the castle only to be killed himself by his lady, in remorse at her betrayal, who then commits suicide.

Above: Alnwick's motte was replaced by a stone shell keep and curtain walls in the first half of the twelfth century and in the fourteenth century its new Percy owners greatly increased its strength, adding towers to the keep, a more formidable gate-house and much more. It was then left virtually unchanged until the eighteenth century when Robert Adam and others did work to convert the keep into a true mansion house. The present appearance owes still more, however, to the 4th Duke of Northumberland and his architect Anthony Salvin who carried out an extensive rebuilding in the nineteenth century.

Right: A keep probably built in the twelfth century during Stephen's reign is the oldest part that now exists of Bamburgh Castle on England's northeast coast, though the site was certainly occupied and probably fortified in Anglo-Saxon times. The rest of the castle was principally built under King John and Henry III. It was besieged twice during the Wars of the Roses, falling the second time in 1464 to Warwick the Kingmaker. It was extensively restored at the end of the nineteenth century by its then owner, the armaments magnate Lord Armstrong.

Above: Hermitage Castle in the Scottish borders. The present structure is a tower house made by building in a fourteenth century courtyard and adapting it for gun defense. Hermitage was a stronghold of the powerful and turbulent Hepburn family. James Hepburn, 4th Earl of Bothwell, was visited here by Mary, Queen of Scots in 1566. In 1567 her husband Henry, Lord Darnley was murdered, possibly with the involvement of Bothwell, who subsequently abducted the widowed Queen and forced her to marry him.

Above: Caerlaverock Castle in southwest Scotland has an unusual triangular plan, dating in this form from 1277. Much of the surviving walls and towers are later – from the fifteenth century – and buildings inside date from the seventeenth century. The tower nearest the camera is known as Murdoch's Tower. Caerlaverock was besieged and taken by the English in 1300 and held until 1312.

Above: Chepstow Castle in Gwent is sited on a cliff above the River Wye controlling one of the main routes between England and south Wales. The earliest part of the castle was built by William fitz Osbern late in the eleventh century, and various other sections were added over the following 200 years, including a great gate built in the 1230s or 1240s, and a D-shaped tower, known as Marten's Tower built by the then owner Roger Bigod during the reign of Edward I late in the thirteenth century. Marten's Tower appears at left in this photograph. Note particularly the spurs projecting from the base of the tower to widen it and provided additional strength against mining, by then a favored siege technique.

Above: Criccieth in Gwynedd, North Wales was taken by Edward I but most of the building on the site had already been erected by the castle's Welsh former owners. The drum towers shown in the photograph were heightened under Edward, at a cost of £318, far less than the expense of building a new castle.

Left: Rhuddlan in Clwyd was one of the first castles built by Edward I in Wales and was begun following his first campaign in 1277. It is built on a concentric plan and includes a fortified dock on the River Clwyd below. Like Edward's other castles in Wales, the work was designed and managed by James of St George. It took a total of nine years to build the castle but most of the work was done in the first four years.

Above: Dunluce Castle in County Antrim in Northern Ireland is perched on the edge of a rocky promontory. The bridge that 'joins' it to the mainland can be seen at the left of the picture. It is no surprise to learn that this was once a drawbridge. The surviving buildings at Dunluce include fourteenth century towers and the remains of a sixteenth century house. The precarious nature of the site was emphasized when part of the castle kitchen fell off over the cliff during a storm in 1639. Perhaps this was why the owner, the 2nd Earl of Antrim, decided, when he returned to possession of his property after the Restoration, to live on the mainland and let the old castle fall into decay.

Above: Bunratty Castle in County Clare in Ireland. Bunratty was built around 1450 for the O'Brien Earls of Thomond. Its most distinctive feature is the deep-set entrance between towers, shown clearly in the photograph.

Above: Carrickfergus, County Antrim, Northern Ireland. Carrickfergus Castle was largely built during the twelfth and thirteenth centuries as an expression of the new English lordship established by John de Courcy in the area in the 1180s. The castle, port (the castle is set by the sea on Belfast Lough) and town of Carrickfergus were all founded together. The photograph shows the gate-house. Originally there would have been a portcullis defending the gate passage which also featured a murder hole.

A NOBLE RESIDENCE

The first castles, relatively inexpensive, fairly small, and constructed of wood, owed everything in their design to military needs with little heed paid to comfort or amenity for those who lived in them and provided their garrisons. As they were replaced with larger and more elaborate stone structures so their internal design also became more sophisticated. There would always be a great hall, but where once it would have fulfilled every domestic and public function from kitchen, bedroom, and dining room to court house and council chamber, later other rooms would be added to perform these roles individually. One common feature soon developed was for the ruling family to have its own apartments, often on a separate floor, both for privacy and for security against treachery from within and as a final stronghold under attack from without.

The first castles were built to defend against foreign raiders, in western Europe notably the Vikings, but such raids came to an end in time and government in many societies became more regular with less likelihood of sudden war. The military service owed by lords and knights to their rulers came to be expressed in money and taxes in the same way that the military functions of their castles became less significant. Other influences made themselves felt on what had once been a society dominated by brash, boorish and violent illiterates. Trade and commerce brought new wealth and new products; women and learning played a more significant role and brought different values to public and private life.

Castles changed under all these influences. From the fifteenth and sixteenth centuries many had more comfortable wings added around a more ancient central structure, albeit perhaps with stout doors and the lowest windows raised significantly above ground level. Others might have draughty stone interiors subdivided and panelled into the more intimate social spaces then becoming customary. Such processes of modernization and extension continued into the modern era.

Other great men preferred, of course, to build anew. Although the military functions of such edifices gradually dwindled to nothing they often still, like the *châteaux* of France, retained the title of castle. Some are marked by their design as simply great houses but others, with lofty sites, turrets, battlements, ditches and moats (albeit purely decorative), rightfully take their place in this account. These visual fantasies of the baroque or Victorian gothic look like castles ought to look and, together with their older renovated and extended cousins, provide a fascinating glimpse of other times and other customs.

Page 93: The first castle at Tattershall in Lincolnshire was built around 1230 with a moat and curtain wall strengthened by towers. The photograph shows the brick-built chamber tower constructed between 1434 and 1446 by Baldwin Docheman for Ralph, Lord Cromwell. Although it is fitted with machicolations, which can be clearly seen in the photograph, and the windows above these are for a rooftop fighting gallery, it is not a serious fortress. It now stands alone on the site but once was joined to a hall. Cromwell had fought at Agincourt and later had an important political career in the government of the young Henry VI. Like Bodiam (see page 79) Tattershall was restored by Lord Curzon.

Pages 94-95: Hever Castle in Kent exhibits two major stages of refurbishment and updating. Much of the gate house at the right of the picture dates from the original thirteenth century structure. The castle passed to the Bullen family in the fifthteenth century and in the years around 1500 they added a comfortable Tudor mansion inside the protective wall and moat. Ann Bullen or Boleyn, second wife of Henry VIII, was a daughter of the family and after her disgrace and execution the property was confiscated and later given to Anne of Cleves, Henry's divorced fourth wife. The second great period of restoration and modernization was from 1903 when the castle was bought by William Waldorf Astor who spent millions restoring the Tudor interior, building a 100-room 'Tudor village' as guest accommodation, and landscaping the gardens and grounds.

Above left: The building of Raby Castle in County Durham was licensed in 1378 but it appears to have been begun earlier in the century. It was owned by the Neville family, including the most famous of the line, Warwick the Kingmaker, of the Wars of the Roses. Long before then Raby had once belonged to King Canute.

Above: The keep of Cardiff Castle. The Romans had one of their Forts of the Saxon Shore here in the fourth century AD. When the Normans arrived they built one of their usual motte and bailey castles on the site, basing the bailey on the same enclosure. The 12-sided shell keep shown in the photograph probably dates from the early twelfth century and the eight-sided tower added on to it (from which the flag flies) is later, probably fifteenth century. The domestic buildings in what was once the bailey (not in picture) are extensive and were greatly restored and rebuilt by the 3rd Marquis of Bute and his architect William Burges in the second half of the nineteenth century.

Above: Arundel was begun shortly after the
Norman conquest on a site above the River
Arun and within view of the south coast. It
was owned for a time by Alice de Louvain,
second wife and later widow of Henry I.
She remarried one William de Albini and he
undertook much building at Arundel. The
shell keep he constructed is regarded as
one of the finest in England and still stands
on its motte at the heart of the castle (the
flag in the photograph is flying from the
thirteenth century tower built onto the shell
keep to defend its entrance). The gate-
house at left is the only other genuinely old
part of the castle which still remains. Much
of the rest was entirely rebuilt in the late
nineteenth century by the then owner the
15th Duke of Norfolk.

Above: Leeds Castle in Kent was
established in the last quarter of the
thirteenth century. It stands on three
islands in an artificial lake made by
damming the River Len. There may
possibly have been a twelfth century
castle on the site previously. Later
construction includes a section built by
Henry VIII. The owner in the early
nineteenth century, Fiennes Wykeham-
Martin, undertook a radical rebuilding,
removing parts of the exterior walls to
create better views of the lake and
restoring the interiors in a supposed
medieval style. One curiosity of the castle's
early days is that it had a water mill.

Above: Belvoir Castle has gone through a whole series of buildings and rebuildings. It was originally an eleventh century motte built for one Robert de Todeni. Updated over the years it was ruined in the Wars of the Roses, again in the Civil War, rebuilt in the later seventeenth century and demolished again in the eighteenth. For much of its history it has been owned by the Earls, later Dukes, of Rutland. Its present form was created for the 5th Duchess in the early nineteenth century by James Wyatt and is a thoroughly exuberant gothic fantasy.

*Above: Eastnor Castle has no pretensions
to antiquity or military utility. It was built for
Lord Somers in 1812-15 by Robert Smirke,
who is better known, perhaps, as the
architect of the British Museum in London.
The interiors were substantially re-worked
later in the nineteenth century by A.W.N.
Pugin.*

Left: Penrhyn Castle with the town of Bangor in the background. By the time Lord Penrhyn came to commission his new castle in Wales, costs had escalated somewhat from the days of Edward I when the area's true castles were built. Penrhyn, built from 1827 to a design in the Norman style by the architect Thomas Hopper, cost its owner half a million pounds. The keep has a similar layout to the original at Rochester.

Above: Eilean Donan Castle on the shores of Loch Duich, built by Alexander II around 1220, was the ancient seat of the Macrae clan. During the brief Jacobite Rebellion of 1719 it was bombarded by Hanoverian warships and completely ruined. The Jacobites had assistance from a small Spanish force, but most of the clans did not join the rising and it was easily defeated at Glen Shiel nearby. Eilean Donan was totally rebuilt in the 1930s to its present highly photogenic outline.

Above: Crathes Castle, just inland from
Aberdeen, was begun in 1553 and largely
completed in 1594. Its various wings and
more generous allocation of windows
reflect a greater attention by this time to
domestic comfort and less to defense. As
well as its fine exterior architecture,
Crathes also boasts an interesting interior,
including a range of superb painted
ceilings.

Right: Thirlstane Castle in Berwickshire in
southeast Scotland. Thirlstane was begun
in 1590 for Maitland of Thirlstane a leading
Scottish politician of the time. It was
substantially re-modeled for the Duke of
Lauderdale, (one of the statesmen who
made up the infamous cabal, Lauderdale
providing the L in that acronym) in 1670-76
by William Bruce and has had various
additions made in the nineteenth century
and since.

Above: From the thirteenth century Dunrobin Castle has been the seat of the earls and later dukes of Sutherland. Robert, the 2nd Earl, built a keep here in about 1275 and some of his stonework is incorporated inside the present buildings. The modern appearance is obviously based on far more recent styles and more generous ideas of comfort. The building was greatly extended by Sir Charles Barry in the nineteenth century and further altered by Sir Robert Lorimer after a fire in 1915 during World War I, when Dunrobin was being used as a military hospital.

Above: The present Inveraray Castle is an eighteenth century replacement for a fifteenth century tower house previously on the site. It has long been the chief home of the heads of the Clan Campbell, the Dukes of Argyll. The present building is principally the work of Robert Mylne and William and John Adam, but the roof line was raised and the dormer windows built in the 1880s. There is a dry moat, but this is practically the only pretence to military purpose. The upper stories were badly damaged by a fire in the 1970s but have since been fully restored.

Above: Drumlanrig is the home of the Dukes of Buccleuch and Queensberry. It was built in 1679-90 for the 1st Duke of Queensberry on the site of a fifteenth century Douglas fortress. The design is in the form of a hollow square with sides of equal length and identical corner towers. Bonnie Prince Charlie spent a night here during his retreat from his invasion of England in the Jacobite Rebellion of 1745-46.

Right: Balmoral Castle on Royal Deeside. Queen Victoria had a lifelong passion for the Scottish Highlands, delighting in the peace and solitude of the scenery and the romance of its historical associations. She and Prince Albert had the castle at Balmoral built in 1853-56 and it still remains the favorite summer holiday destination of most of the royal family.

Overleaf: Floors Castle is the home of the Dukes of Roxburghe. It was designed and built by William Adam in 1721-25 and extensively remodeled by William Playfair in the 1840s. It is the largest and probably the grandest great house in Scotland. James II was killed in 1460 at a spot marked in the grounds of Floors when one of the cannon he was using to besiege Roxburgh accidentally exploded.

Craigievar is said to be the truest specimen of the Scottish tower house. It may owe this reputation in part to two chance occurrences. On the one hand, all the adjacent walls and outbuildings that would once have accompanied it have been removed over the years so that the house itself stands alone clearly to be seen, while on the other hand, the actual house is still virtually as it was when it was completed in 1626. It was built for "Danzig Willie" Forbes, a prosperous merchant in the Baltic trade from nearby Aberdeen. It follows the Scottish penchant for a generally vertical design, building upward rather than spreading outward, with plain lower stories erupting into a plethora of turrets and rooftop decorations. One consequence of this is narrow stairways and it is said that the Forbes family always entered by the door, but in the end would have to leave by a window since no coffin could be maneuvered down the stairs.

Above: Carrick-on-Suir, County Tipperary. As the photograph shows, the castle at Carrick-on-Suir consists of two main parts. There is an older tower which remains from a thirteenth century castle built for the Butlers of Ormond. There is a story that Anne Boleyn (see Hever Castle, pages 94-95) was born here as her family was related to the Butlers. The 10th Earl of Ormond built the second part of the castle, a lavish mansion house, in the reign of Queen Elizabeth, hoping that his sovereign would come to visit, but she never did.

Right: The Alcázar at Segovia, one of the most famous castles in Spain. Following a fire in 1862 which completely gutted the interior, only the walls and towers now stand on an imposing rocky site above the river.

Overleaf: Kylemore Castle in County Galway. Kylemore was built in the nineteenth century in the mock-Tudor style for a Manchester millionaire-turned-politician, Mitchell Henry. He spent millions both on his baronial style palace and on reclaiming surrounding marsh-land to create an estate lavishly decorated with rhododendrons and fuchsia. Since World War I the castle has been a Benedictine convent, accommodating a house displaced from their former residence at Ypres in Belgium by military action.

Left: The Castelo da Pena, Sintra, Portugal. The Castelo da Pena was commissioned by Ferdinand of Saxe-Coburg-Gotha, consort of Maria II of Portugal. (Ferdinand was the cousin of Prince Albert, consort of Queen Victoria. The family seem to have married well and to have had similar tastes in castles.) Castelo da Pena was built on the site of a monastery founded by Manuel I in 1509. The architect of the present building was a Baron von Eschwege who, as the picture shows, built in an elaborate largely gothic style.

Above: Burg Hochosterwitz in Carinthia, Austria. Burg Hochosterwitz was built in 1570-86 by Georg von Khevenhüller on the site of an earlier castle. It sits high on a limestone rock about 160 metres (500 feet) above its valley. To reach into the inner sections of the castle a visitor (or an attacker) has to climb up a spiral approach and pass through 16 gates.

Above: Azay-le-Rideau lies on a little island in a loop of the Indre river in France. An old feudal fortress did stand on the site, but it was burned down in 1418 during the wars with England when the garrison refused to recognize the royal status of the then Dauphin. The building that now exists dates from the early sixteenth century. It was begun by the financier Gilles Berthelot but after he had died in exile in Italy the property was confiscated and given to the commander of the royal guard. The design shows the strong Italian influence over French Renaissance architecture. This is especially seen in the main courtyard (not shown in this photograph). It was not, however, until the nineteenth century and the ownership of the Biencourt family that the château was actually completed. According to the writer Balzac, who lived nearby, Azay with its handsome grounds was a "richly faceted diamond set in the Indre."

Above: The towers of the castle at Angers have a distinctive banded appearance, believed to be inspired by the walls of Constantinople, and achieved by using layers of different types of stone. Angers was built in 1232-38 by Blanche of Castile, Queen Mother and Regent for Louis IX. The towers originally were higher and topped by conical roofs. Because of the strength they gave to the walls, no central keep was built.

Overleaf: The Château de Chambord is the grandest of the many fine châteaux of the Loire region. Its construction was begun by François I in 1515 but was not completely finished by his death in 1547. Although the quadrangular plan is seemingly protected by great drum towers, the large windows and proliferation of chimneys (365 in all), domes and other delicate rooftop decoration show its residential rather than military function. Leonardo da Vinci may have been involved in the building's design, for he was invited to live nearby at Amboise by François for the last years of his (Leonardo's) life. Among the features attributed to Leonardo are the castle's famous double-helix spiral staircase which leads to an ornate roof terrace with fine views over the grounds and the River Cosson, which was diverted during the building's construction (although François had originally wanted to divert the much larger Loire).

Left: The Château d'Amboise overlooking
the Loire river. The château at Amboise
has many royal associations. It was
confiscated from the original owners, the
Amboise family, by Charles VII. Charles
VIII commissioned extensions to the
buildings and died here in 1498 after
striking his head on a low beam while
going to play tennis in the dry moat. (An
alternative tale suggests that he died after
eating a bad orange). The work ordered by
Charles VIII from 1492 was among the first
in France to adopt Italian fashions.
François I also lived here in his youth. Few
of the Renaissance buildings now remain,
however, as much was demolished at the
start of the nineteenth century. In 1560,
after a Huguenot plot against the young
King François II was foiled, several
hundred of the plot's supporters were
executed at Amboise while the royal court
watched from the windows. Among those
present were the young king and his wife,
Mary, Queen of Scots. The bodies were
afterwards hung from the battlements
before being thrown into the Loire in sacks.

Above: The Château de Cheverny was
built between 1604 and 1634 and is still
owned by descendants of the Comte de
Cheverny who built it. This photograph of
the main façade emphasizes the
symmetrical layout with the simple
entrance being flanked by paired roofs,
chimneys, domes and lanterns. An
important interest of the château's owners
throughout the years has been hunting.
There is a notable trophy room and the
daily soupe des chiens when the dogs are
fed is still an attraction for visitors.

Left: The Château de Langeais has a dual character. The section overlooking the garden, as shown in the photograph, has larger windows and decorative stonework, while facing the town there are machicolations and a drawbridge. The present buildings date from 1470 and originally performed a strategic function on the borders between Brittany and France. The construction was managed by Jean Bourré, financial secretary to Louis XI and then to his successors Charles VIII and Louis XII. The marriage of Charles VIII and Anne of Brittany which ended the potential conflict between France and Brittany was sealed here in 1491. Also on the site is a ruined donjon dating back to 944 which is the oldest in France and probably, in effect, one of the oldest castles in the world.

Overleaf: The Château de Josselin overlooks the River Oust in Brittany. It has the remains of nine cylindrical towers, the three most complete rising directly from the rocky river bank. Josselin has been subject to various demolitions over the years. It was bought in 1370 by the Constable of France, Olivier de Clisson. The de Rohan family who subsequently owned it took the French side against the reigning Duke François II of Brittany and in 1488 he ordered Josselin dismantled. The marriages of Anne of Brittany that united the duchy to the French kingdom brought the de Rohan's back into favor and Jean de Rohan commissioned work early in the sixteenth century to make it into a more comfortable country mansion. In 1629 it was time for another dismantling when the king's chief minister Cardinal Richelieu had the donjon blown up and most of the towers demolished. Extensive nineteenth century restoration completes the picture.

Acknowledgments
The author and publisher would like to thank Judith Millidge the editor, Suzanne O'Farrell the picture researcher, Design 23 the designers, and Simon Shelmerdine for production. The following individuals and institutions have granted permission for use of the photographs on the pages noted below:

AA PICTURE LIBRARY 2-3, 17, 22, 26, 28, 30, 35, 38, 41, 43, 46, 48-49, 51, 58, 61, 63, 67, 68, 69, 78, 81, 83, 86, 90, 93, 94-5, 96, 97, 100, 105, 107, 108, 109, 110-111, 112-13, 114, 116-17, 126-27, 128.

A F KERSTING 12-13, 14, 18, 23, 24-5, 34-5, 52, 53, 59, 60, 62, 64, 71, 72-3, 74, 75, 76, 80, 84, 85, 98, 99.

CAROLINE JONES 44-45, 79.

LIFE FILE © Tony Abbott 29, 118; © Ron Bonser 5; © Ian Booth 20-21, 50; © Graham Buchan 77; © Dr R Cannon 27; © Sue Davis 115; © Mike Evans 56 (both); © Caroline Field 57, 91, 104; © Tim Fisher 66; © Jeremy Hoare 54; © C Klein 121; © Emma Lee 11, 31, 101; © Mike Maidment 55; © Louise Oldroyd 32; © Richard Power 1, 36, 37; © F Ralson 7; © Paul Richards 106; © Nigel Shuttleworth 82; © Eddy Tan 19, 119; © Cliff Threadgold 87, 89; © David Toase 16, 88, 102; © Flora Torrance39, 47; © Terence Waeland 125; © Andrew Ward 8, 9, 42, 65, 103, 120, 122-23, 124; © Eric Wilkins 4, 15.